The Importance of Reading Fluency

by Gerald Tindal, Ph.D.

Struggling readers, in general, lack fluency. Therefore, attention to fluency instruction should be a major component of any reading program.

As defined by the National Reading Panel (2000), fluency is "reading text with speed, accuracy, and proper expression." Fluent readers are like musicians or athletes who no longer have to "think" about a behavior; they "just do it." A fluent reader moves over the words, sequencing them effortlessly, providing appropriate intonation, and integrating the punctuation. Fluent reading is easily discerned by the reader's audience.

The importance of reading fluency cannot be underestimated, or its relevance doubted. Comprehension improves when students read quickly, accurately, and smoothly. Jay Samuels, of the University of Minnesota, used the term *automaticity* to describe the relationship between decoding and comprehension. Basically, when students become fluent, decoding is automatic and no cognitive effort is needed to read; the result is a nearly total focus on comprehension.

Additionally, there are some major side benefits of fluency instruction. As students become more fluent readers, they can begin to command their own learning and participate more broadly in the language community. With reading fluency comes greater awareness of the world and opportunity to interact with others, allowing students to help each other practice, rehearse for performances, and share their skills with an audience.

Enjoy helping your students move toward reading fluency!

Dr. Tindal is the Castle-McIntosh-Knight Professor of Education at the University of Oregon in Eugene, Oregon.

Teaching Fluency

In order for students to become fluent readers, they need to have oral reading modeled for them; they need repeated oral reading practice; and they benefit greatly from performing their oral reading.

MODELING ORAL READING

Use the overhead transparencies in this book to demonstrate various qualities of fluent oral reading: rate, phrasing, and intonation. (More about using the transparencies appears on page 4.)

Rate

Explain to students that oral reading rate varies depending on the type of selection being read.

- A faster rate is appropriate for lighthearted pieces such as riddles, jokes, tongue twisters, and limericks.

- A slower rate will better convey meaning when reading nonfiction selections or folk tales and myths.

- Readers' Theater should be read at a rate that corresponds with spoken dialogue.

Phrasing

Explain the importance of reading in phrases, rather than word by word. Use the transparencies to demonstrate how to divide text into meaningful chunks (see page 4).

Intonation

Intonation is the distinctive tone of voice that conveys meaning. Guide students to scan ahead for punctuation that signals appropriate intonation.

- A question mark signals the reader to end the sentence with a slightly higher voice.

- An exclamation mark indicates words that should be read with strong feeling.

- Words in quotation marks should be read as if they are being spoken.

Building Fluency • EMC 3341 • © Evan-Moor Corp.

PRACTICING ORAL READING

Keep fluency practice fun and interesting by using a variety of techniques, such as those explained below. Older students may have their own ideas about ways to enliven practice.

Choral Reading

Choral reading is simply reading in unison. Enliven your fluency practice by trying a number of approaches to choral reading throughout the year:

- Refrain reading—one student reads most of the piece and the rest of the class reads repeated sections.

- Antiphonal reading—small groups of students are each assigned a different section of text. One group reads its part, and a different group reads another part, such as the chorus or refrain. This technique is effective with chants, songs, and poems.

- Radio reading—small groups of four to six students are assigned a passage of text. Each student reads a part of the passage in the proper order. This technique is perfect for speeches, nonfiction, and tales, myths, and legends.

- Call and response—one student reads part of a joke or riddle, for example, and the whole group responds by reading the punch line or answer.

- Cumulative—one child or small group begins the reading and is sequentially joined by one or more readers until the entire class is reading.

Partner Reading

In partner reading, one student reads a line or a part, and the partner reads the next line or part.

Echo Reading

In echo reading, a proficient reader is paired with a less proficient reader. The better reader reads one sentence or phrase. The other reader echoes back, following along with a finger.

PERFORMING ORAL READING

A performance celebrates the fluency achieved by daily practice. Friday afternoons are a perfect time for your readers to strut their stuff. Invite a buddy class or someone special, such as the principal, to share in the fun!

Using the Transparencies

The Transparencies

Twenty selections from this book are provided on transparencies to assist you in modeling appropriate rate, phrasing, and intonation for students. These selections are also indicated in the Table of Contents for each section of the book.

Demonstrating Phrasing on the Transparencies

Fluent readers divide text into meaningful "chunks," rather than reading word by word. For example, when a fluent reader reads the sentence "Slue-Foot Sue **/** was one of the greatest ladies **/** of the Texas frontier," he or she would automatically pause as indicated by the slash marks.

Demonstrate how to cluster words together by making slash marks (**/**) with a marking pen on a chosen transparency. Read the selection to the students, and then read chorally as a group. Practice several times, with and without the slash marks.

Starting below and continuing through page 6, you will find reductions of the transparency selections showing suggested markings for phrasing.

Page 13

Page 14

Page 19

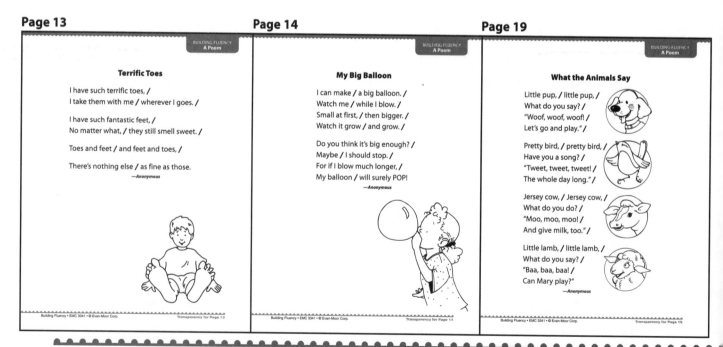

Terrific Toes

I have such terrific toes, /
I take them with me / wherever I goes. /

I have such fantastic feet, /
No matter what, / they still smell sweet. /

Toes and feet / and feet and toes, /

There's nothing else / as fine as those.
—*Anonymous*

My Big Balloon

I can make / a big balloon. /
Watch me / while I blow. /
Small at first, / then bigger. /
Watch it grow / and grow. /

Do you think it's big enough? /
Maybe / I should stop. /
For if I blow much longer, /
My balloon / will surely POP!
—*Anonymous*

What the Animals Say

Little pup, / little pup, /
What do you say? /
"Woof, woof, woof! /
Let's go and play." /

Pretty bird, / pretty bird, /
Have you a song? /
"Tweet, tweet, tweet! /
The whole day long." /

Jersey cow, / Jersey cow, /
What do you do? /
"Moo, moo, moo! /
And give milk, too." /

Little lamb, / little lamb, /
What do you say? /
"Baa, baa, baa! /
Can Mary play?"
—*Anonymous*

BUILDING FLUENCY
A Poem

Five Little Owls

Five little owls / in an old elm tree, /
Fluffy and puffy / as owls could be. /
Blinking and winking / with big round eyes /
At the big round moon / that hung in the skies. /

As I passed by, / I could hear one say, /
"There will be mouse for supper, /
There will, / today!" /

Then all of them hooted, /
"Tu-whit, / tu-whoo, /
Yes, / mouse for supper, /
Hoo, hoo, hoo, hoo!"

—*Anonymous*

Building Fluency • EMC 3341 • © Evan-Moor Corp.   Transparency for Page 21

BUILDING FLUENCY
A Poem

Once I Saw a Little Bird

Once I saw / a little bird /
Come and hop, hop, hop. /
And I cried, "Little bird, /
Will you stop, stop, stop?" /

I was going to the window /
To say, / "How do you do?" /
But he shook his little tail, /
And far away / he flew.

—*Anonymous*

Building Fluency • EMC 3341 • © Evan-Moor Corp.   Transparency for Page 22

BUILDING FLUENCY
A Poem

Rags

I have a dog /
And his name is Rags. /

He eats so much /
That his tummy sags. /

His ears flip-flop, /
And his tail wig-wags. /

And when he walks, /
He goes zig-zag.

—*Anonymous*

Building Fluency • EMC 3341 • © Evan-Moor Corp.   Transparency for Page 24

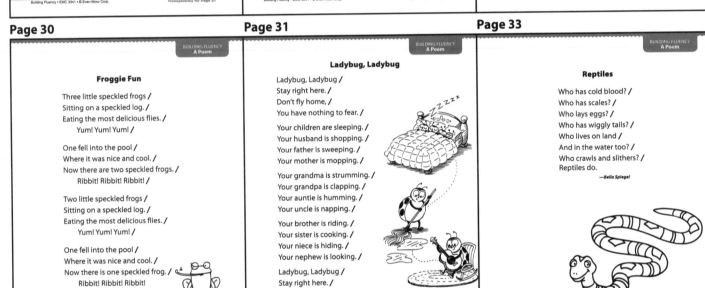

BUILDING FLUENCY
A Poem

Froggie Fun

Three little speckled frogs /
Sitting on a speckled log. /
Eating the most delicious flies. /
　Yum! Yum! Yum! /

One fell into the pool /
Where it was nice and cool. /
Now there are two speckled frogs. /
　Ribbit! Ribbit! Ribbit! /

Two little speckled frogs /
Sitting on a speckled log. /
Eating the most delicious flies. /
　Yum! Yum! Yum! /

One fell into the pool /
Where it was nice and cool. /
Now there is one speckled frog. /
　Ribbit! Ribbit! Ribbit!

—*Anonymous*

Building Fluency • EMC 3341 • © Evan-Moor Corp.   Transparency for Page 30

BUILDING FLUENCY
A Poem

Ladybug, Ladybug

Ladybug, Ladybug /
Stay right here. /
Don't fly home, /
You have nothing to fear. /

Your children are sleeping. /
Your husband is shopping. /
Your father is sweeping. /
Your mother is mopping. /

Your grandma is strumming. /
Your grandpa is clapping. /
Your auntie is humming. /
Your uncle is napping. /

Your brother is riding. /
Your sister is cooking. /
Your niece is hiding. /
Your nephew is looking. /

Ladybug, Ladybug /
Stay right here. /
Don't fly home, /
You have nothing to fear.

—*John Himmelman*

Building Fluency • EMC 3341 • © Evan-Moor Corp.   Transparency for Page 31

BUILDING FLUENCY
A Poem

Reptiles

Who has cold blood? /
Who has scales? /
Who lays eggs? /
Who has wiggly tails? /
Who lives on land /
And in the water too? /
Who crawls and slithers? /
Reptiles do.

—*Bella Spiegel*

Building Fluency • EMC 3341 • © Evan-Moor Corp.   Transparency for Page 33

BUILDING FLUENCY
A Song

My Country, 'Tis of Thee

My country, / 'tis of thee, /
Sweet land of liberty, /
Of thee / I sing; /
Land where my fathers died, /
Land of the pilgrims' pride, /
From every mountainside, /
Let freedom ring.

—*Samuel F. Smith*

Building Fluency • EMC 3341 • © Evan-Moor Corp.   Transparency for Page 36

BUILDING FLUENCY
A Chant

Did You Feed My Cow?

Did you feed my cow? /
　Yes, Ma'am! /
Will you tell me how? /
　Yes, Ma'am! /

Oh, / what did you give her? /
　Corn and hay. /
Oh, / what did you give her? /
　Corn and hay. /

Did you milk her good? /
　Yes, Ma'am! /
Did you do / like you should? /
　Yes, Ma'am! /

Oh, / how did you milk her? /
　Swish! Swish! Swish! /
Oh, / how did you milk her? /
　Swish! Swish! Swish!

—*Anonymous*

Building Fluency • EMC 3341 • © Evan-Moor Corp.   Transparency for Page 41

BUILDING FLUENCY
A Rhyme

The Three Little Kittens

Three little kittens / lost their mittens, /
And they began to cry, /
"Oh! / Mother dear, / we greatly fear, /
Our mittens / we have lost." /

"What! / Lost your mittens? /
You naughty kittens. /
Then / you shall have no pie!" /

"Meow, meow, meow, /
We shall have no pie." /

Three little kittens / found their mittens, /
And they began to cry, /
"Oh! / Mother dear, / see here, / see here, /
Our mittens / we have found." /

"What! / Found your mittens? /
You good little kittens. /
Then / you shall have some pie." /

"Meow, meow, meow, /
We shall have some pie!"

—*Anonymous*

Building Fluency • EMC 3341 • © Evan-Moor Corp.   Transparency for Page 48

The Bath

Sam dug / in the mud. /
He had fun. /
Sam is a mess. /
He must get a bath. /
Sam did not want a bath. /
He ran and ran. /
Mom got Sam. /
Sam got a bath. /
Now / Sam is not a mess. /
Sam gets a bone.

The Polar Bear

The polar bear / lives near the North Pole. /
Every day, / it walks on the snow. /
It has fur / on the bottom / of its feet. /
The fur / keeps its feet warm. /
It also keeps the bear / from slipping on the snow. /

Every day, / the polar bear swims in the cold water. /
The polar bear / is a good swimmer. /
It paddles / with its front legs. /
It pulls its back legs along. /

After it swims, / it shakes the water / from its fur coat. /
BRRRR!

Good Morning!

Wake up! / It's morning. / What do you see? /
The sun in the sky /
And the birds in a tree. /

Wake up! / It's morning. / What do you hear? /
Someone is singing /
A song / soft and clear. /

Wake up! / It's morning. / What do you hold? /
The covers around me /
To keep out the cold. /

Wake up! / It's morning. / What do you smell? /
Someone is frying
An egg, / I can tell. /

Wake up! / It's morning. / What do you eat? /
Warm oats and cold milk, /
And berries so sweet.

Weather Helps Us

Look outside. /
What do you see? /
Wind / is blowing in the tree. /

Wind helps us. /
It makes sailboats move. /
It makes kites fly high. /

Look outside. /
What do you see? /
Rain / is falling on the tree. /

Rain helps us. /
Rain fills lakes and rivers / with good water. /
Plants need water / to live and grow. /

Look outside. /
What do you see? /
The sun / is shining on the tree. /

The sun helps us. /
Plants, / animals, / and people / all need sunshine. /
The sun helps plants grow. /
People and animals / eat plants.

Run, Swim, Fly

Do you ever watch animals move? /
If you do, / you will see them move / in may ways. /

Animals on land may walk, / run, / jump, / or hop. /
Some, / like snakes or snails, / crawl. /

Bats and most birds fly. /
Insects / like bees and ladybugs / fly, too. /

Fish and whales / live in the water. /
Most animals / that live in water / swim.

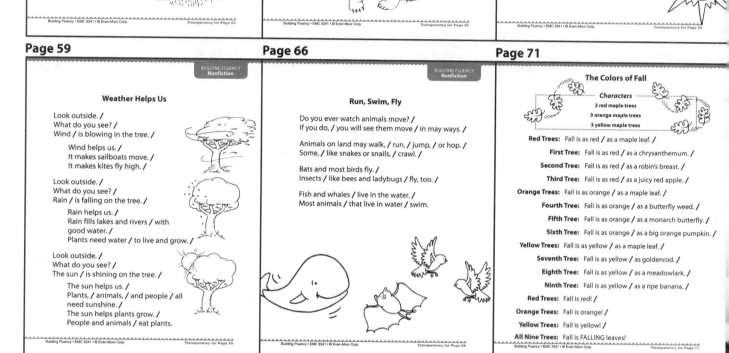

The Colors of Fall

Characters
3 red maple trees
3 orange maple trees
3 yellow maple trees

Red Trees: Fall is as red / as a maple leaf. /
First Tree: Fall is as red / as a chrysanthemum. /
Second Tree: Fall is as red / as a robin's breast. /
Third Tree: Fall is as red / as a juicy red apple. /
Orange Trees: Fall is as orange / as a maple leaf. /
Fourth Tree: Fall is as orange / as a butterfly weed. /
Fifth Tree: Fall is as orange / as a monarch butterfly. /
Sixth Tree: Fall is as orange / as a big orange pumpkin. /
Yellow Trees: Fall is as yellow / as a maple leaf. /
Seventh Tree: Fall is as yellow / as goldenrod. /
Eighth Tree: Fall is as yellow / as a meadowlark. /
Ninth Tree: Fall is as yellow / as a ripe banana. /
Red Trees: Fall is red! /
Orange Trees: Fall is orange! /
Yellow Trees: Fall is yellow! /
All Nine Trees: Fall is FALLING leaves!

Jack and the Beanstalk
by Judith Gold and Carrie Mapes

Characters

Reader 1	Reader 2
Reader 3	Reader 4

Reader 1: For Jack and his mother, / the times were bad, /
So Jack took magic beans / for the only cow they had. /

Reader 2: Jack's mother was angry / and threw with all of her might. / The beans went out the window, / and she went to bed / for the night. /

Reader 3: Next morning, / Jack woke up / to find an awesome sight. / A beanstalk had sprouted / where the beans lay last night! /

Reader 4: Jack looked up, up, up, / as high as eagles fly. / He saw that the beanstalk / stretched to the sky. /

Reader 1: Jack climbed the beanstalk / as quick as a mouse. / There at the top / stood a huge stone house! /

Reader 2: Inside the castle, / Jack crept all around. / He spied a fearsome giant / whose voice shook the ground. /

Reader 3: "Fe, / fi, / fo, / fum!" / yelled the giant / with an angry face. / Jack jumped in the oven. / What a good hiding place! /

Reader 4: From there, / Jack saw gold. / And since the giant was asleep, / Jack ran home fast. / The coins were his to keep. /

Reader 1: Jack and his mom / spent the coins. / None remain. / So Jack had to climb / to the castle again. /

Reader 2: Jack crawled through the kitchen, / between the / table legs. / On the table was a hen / laying golden eggs. /

Reader 3: Jack grabbed the hen / and made it home without a hitch. / With golden eggs to buy things, / now they were rich. /

Reader 4: Again Jack climbed the beanstalk, / which wasn't too wise. / He snatched up a harp / as his last golden prize. /

Reader 1: As Jack snuck away, / the giant woke and said, / "I'll catch that little thief! / His bones / will make / my bread!" /

Reader 2: The giant gave chase. / Down the beanstalk / Jack ran fast. / He saw his mother / and his ax at last. /

Reader 3: In the nick of time, / Jack made it back. / He swung at the beanstalk / with a mighty whack. /

Reader 4: The giant fell down / and Jack laughed with glee. / So Jack and his mother / lived ever after happily.

Poetry

Page 12 Walking, Walking

Page 13 Terrific Toes*

Page 14 My Big Balloon*

Page 15 Bubble, Bubble

Page 16 Thank You

Page 17 Mix a Pancake

Page 18 Bubble Gum

Page 19 What the Animals Say*

Page 20 Good Morning, Mrs. Hen

Page 21 Five Little Owls*

Page 22 What's for Lunch?

Page 23 Once I Saw a Little Bird*

Page 24 Rags*

Page 25 Five Furry Kittens

Page 26 Little Monkeys

Page 27 One Gorilla

Page 28 Giant Tortoise

Page 29 Spring Is Coming

Page 30 Froggie Fun*

✳ **Page 31** Ladybug, Ladybug*

Page 32 Zip, Zoom

Page 33 Reptiles*

✳ **Page 34** Flying High

* Transparency provided

Walking, Walking

Walking, walking,
walking, walking.

Hop, hop, hop,
hop, hop, hop.

Running, running, running,
running, running, running.

Now let's stop,
now let's stop.

—*Anonymous*

Terrific Toes

I have such terrific toes,
I take them with me wherever I goes.

I have such fantastic feet,
No matter what, they still smell sweet.

Toes and feet and feet and toes,
There's nothing else as fine as those.

—*Anonymous*

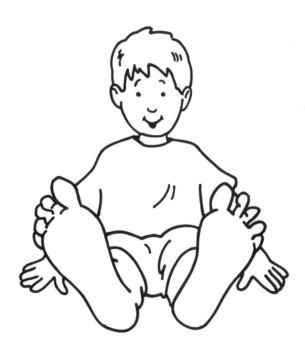

My Big Balloon

I can make a big balloon.
Watch me while I blow.
Small at first, then bigger.
Watch it grow and grow.

Do you think it's big enough?
Maybe I should stop.
For if I blow much longer,
My balloon will surely POP!

—*Anonymous*

Name _____

Mix a Pancake

Mix a pancake,

Stir a pancake,

    Pop it in the pan;

Fry the pancake,

Toss the pancake,

    Catch it if you can.

—*Christina G. Rossetti*

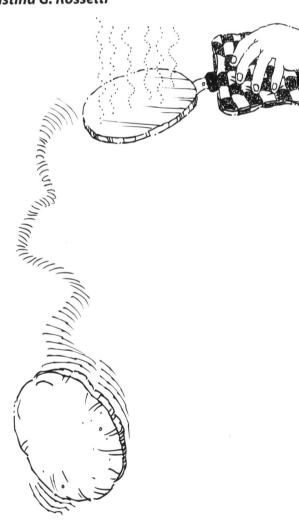

Bubble Gum

Bubble gum, bubble gum,
chew and blow.

Bubble gum, bubble gum,
scrape your toe.

Bubble gum, bubble gum,
tastes so sweet.

Get that bubble gum
off your feet!

—*Anonymous*

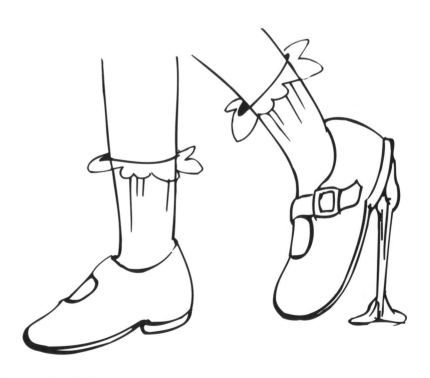

Name _____

What the Animals Say

Little pup, little pup,
What do you say?
"Woof, woof, woof!
Let's go and play."

Pretty bird, pretty bird,
Have you a song?
"Tweet, tweet, tweet!
The whole day long."

Jersey cow, Jersey cow,
What do you do?
"Moo, moo, moo!
And give milk, too."

Little lamb, little lamb,
What do you say?
"Baa, baa, baa!
Can Mary play?"

—*Anonymous*

Good Morning, Mrs. Hen

Good morning, Mrs. Hen.
How many chickens have you got?

Madam, I've got ten;
Four of them yellow,
Four of them brown,
And two of them are speckled red,
The nicest in the town.

—*Anonymous*

Five Little Owls

Five little owls in an old elm tree,
Fluffy and puffy as owls could be.
Blinking and winking with big round eyes
At the big round moon that hung in the skies.

As I passed by, I could hear one say,
"There will be mouse for supper,
There will, today!"

Then all of them hooted,
"Tu-whit, tu-whoo,
Yes, mouse for supper,
Hoo, hoo, hoo, hoo!"

—*Anonymous*

What's for Lunch?

I have a goat.
What a funny pet.
He'll eat anything
He can get.

    crunchy hay
    modeling clay
    Grandpa's socks
    moss on rocks
    leaves on trees
    beans and peas
    labels on cans
    greasy pans

Watch him lick.
Watch him munch.
He thinks anything's
A good lunch.

          —Anonymous

Once I Saw a Little Bird

Once I saw a little bird
Come and hop, hop, hop.
And I cried, "Little bird,
Will you stop, stop, stop?"

I was going to the window
To say, "How do you do?"
But he shook his little tail,
And far away he flew.

—*Anonymous*

Rags

I have a dog
And his name is Rags.

He eats so much
That his tummy sags.

His ears flip-flop,
And his tail wig-wags.

And when he walks,
He goes zig-zag.

—*Anonymous*

Name _____

Five Furry Kittens

Five furry kittens one spring night
sat on a fence. What a funny sight!

The first one danced
on her kitty toes.

The second one washed
his little black nose.

The third one turned
around and around.

The fourth one jumped
down to the ground.

The fifth one sang
a kitty song.

Five furry kittens
played all night long.

—*Anonymous*

Little Monkeys

Four little monkeys sitting in a tree

Teasing Mr. Crocodile—"You can't catch me."

Along comes Mr. Crocodile

As quiet as can be—SNAP!

Three little monkeys sitting in a tree

Teasing Mr. Crocodile—"You can't catch me."

Along comes Mr. Crocodile

As quiet as can be—SNAP!

Two little monkeys sitting in a tree

Teasing Mr. Crocodile—"You can't catch me."

Along comes Mr. Crocodile

As quiet as can be—SNAP!

One little monkey sitting in a tree

Teasing Mr. Crocodile—"You can't catch me."

Along comes Mr. Crocodile

As quiet as can be—SNAP!

Away swims Mr. Crocodile

As full as he can be!

—Anonymous

One Gorilla

One Gorilla,
Two Gorillas,
Three Gorillas,
Four.

Five Gorillas,
Six Gorillas,
Seven Gorillas
Snore.

Eight Gorillas,
Nine Gorillas,
Ten Gorillas
Roar.

Ten little gorillas
in a syc-a-more!

—*Anonymous*

Giant Tortoise

Step by step—see it go.
Step by step—soooo slow.

Heavy shell on its back
Heavy shell—like a pack.

Plodding on in the sand.
Plodding on over land.

Step by step—see it go.
Step by step—soooo slow.

—*Anonymous*

Name _____

Reptiles

Who has cold blood?

Who has scales?

Who lays eggs?

Who has wiggly tails?

Who lives on land

And in the water too?

Who crawls and slithers?

Reptiles do.

—*Bella Spiegel*

Name _____

Flying High

I watch the birds fly high.
I watch the birds fly low.
It's always fun to watch them.
They put on quite a show.

If I just had some wings,
I'd soar into the blue.
I'd circle, swoop, and dive.
Would you find that fun, too?

—*Jo Ellen Moore*

Songs, Chants, and Rhymes

Songs

Page 36 My Country, 'Tis of Thee*

Page 37 Old MacDonald

Page 39 Bingo
Oh Where, Oh Where Has My
   Little Dog Gone?

Chants

Page 40 Peanut Butter and Jelly

Page 41 Did You Feed My Cow?*

Rhymes

Page 42 Silly Sailor
Rain

Page 43 Pease Porridge

Page 44 One, Two

Page 45 Mabel

Page 46 Little Bo Peep
Diddle, Diddle, Dumpling

Page 47 To Market, To Market
Hey Diddle, Diddle

Page 48 The Three Little Kittens*

Page 49 Old Mother Hubbard

Page 50 Rattlesnake
Boa, Boa

* Transparency provided

My Country, 'Tis of Thee

My country, 'tis of thee,

Sweet land of liberty,

Of thee I sing;

Land where my fathers died,

Land of the pilgrims' pride,

From every mountainside,

Let freedom ring.

—*Samuel F. Smith*

Name _____

Old MacDonald

Old MacDonald had a farm, ee-ii-ee-ii-oo!
And on that farm he had some ducks,
    ee-ii-ee-ii-oo!
    With a quack, quack here
    and a quack, quack there,
    here a quack, there a quack,
    everywhere a quack, quack.
Old MacDonald had a farm, ee-ii-ee-ii-oo!

Old MacDonald had a farm, ee-ii-ee-ii-oo!
And on that farm he had some pigs,
   ee-ii-ee-ii-oo!
   With an oink, oink here
   and an oink, oink there,
   here an oink, there an oink,
   everywhere an oink, oink.
Old MacDonald had a farm, ee-ii-ee-ii-oo!

Old MacDonald had a farm, ee-ii-ee-ii-oo!
And on that farm he had some sheep,
   ee-ii-ee-ii-oo!
   With a baa, baa here
   and a baa, baa there,
   here a baa, there a baa,
   everywhere a baa, baa.
Old MacDonald had a farm, ee-ii-ee-ii-oo!

Old MacDonald had a farm, ee-ii-ee-ii-oo!
And on that farm he had some horses,
   ee-ii-ee-ii-oo!
   With a neigh, neigh here
   and a neigh, neigh there,
   here a neigh, there a neigh,
   everywhere a neigh, neigh.
Old MacDonald had a farm, ee-ii-ee-ii-oo!

—Anonymous

Name _____

Bingo

There was a farmer had a dog
and Bingo was his name-o.
B - I - N - G - O, B - I - N - G - O, B - I - N - G - O
And Bingo was his name-o.

—Anonymous

Oh Where, Oh Where
Has My Little Dog Gone?

Oh where, oh where has my little dog gone?
Oh where, oh where can he be?

With his ears cut short and his tail cut long,
Oh where, oh where can he be?

—Anonymous

Peanut Butter and Jelly

First you take the dough and knead it, knead it.
Peanut butter, peanut butter, jelly, jelly.

Then you pop it in the oven and bake it, bake it.
Peanut butter, peanut butter, jelly, jelly.

Then you take a knife and slice it, slice it.
Peanut butter, peanut butter, jelly, jelly.

Then you take the peanuts and mash them, mash them.
Peanut butter, peanut butter, jelly, jelly.

Then you take a knife and spread it, spread it.
Peanut butter, peanut butter, jelly, jelly.

Then you take the grapes and squash them, squash them.
Peanut butter, peanut butter, jelly, jelly.

Then you glop it on the bread and smear it, smear it.
Peanut butter, peanut butter, jelly, jelly.

Then you take the sandwich and eat it, eat it.
Peanut butter, peanut butter, jelly, jelly.

—*Anonymous*

Did You Feed My Cow?

Did you feed my cow?
 Yes, Ma'am!
Will you tell me how?
 Yes, Ma'am!

Oh, what did you give her?
 Corn and hay.
Oh, what did you give her?
 Corn and hay.

Did you milk her good?
 Yes, Ma'am!
Did you do like you should?
 Yes, Ma'am!

Oh, how did you milk her?
 Swish! Swish! Swish!
Oh, how did you milk her?
 Swish! Swish! Swish!

     —Anonymous

Silly Sailor

A sailor went to sea sea sea,
To see what he could see see see,
But all that he could see see see,
Was the bottom of the deep blue sea sea sea.

—*Anonymous*

Rain

Rain on the green grass,
And rain on the tree,
And rain on the housetop,
But not on me.

—*Anonymous*

Fiction and Nonfiction

Page 52 At the Pond

Page 53 The Bath*

Page 54 The Lost Tooth

Page 55 The Polar Bear*

Page 56 The Weather

Page 57 Story of the Year

Page 58 Good Morning!*

Page 59 Weather Helps Us*

Page 60 Sing While You Wash

Page 61 Where You Live

Page 62 Chicken Licken

Page 65 The Lion and the Mouse

Page 66 Run, Swim, Fly*

Page 67 Country Mouse and City Mouse

* Transparency provided

Name _____

At the Pond

The pond is big.
A log is in the pond.
A frog is on the log.

The frog can see a bug.
Can the frog get the bug?
It does get the bug.

My dog runs to the pond.
He can see the frog.
Can he get the frog?

My dog did not get the frog.
The frog is fast.
My dog is wet!

Name _____

The Bath

Sam dug in the mud.
He had fun.

Sam is a mess.
He must get a bath.

Sam did not want a bath.
He ran and ran.

Mom got Sam.
Sam got a bath.

Now Sam is not a mess.
Sam gets a bone.

Name _____

The Lost Tooth

You won't believe what happened.
It really was a surprise.

I opened my mouth.
I couldn't believe my eyes.

My tooth was hanging loose,
Just holding at one side.

I could push it back and forth.
I really was terrified.

It wiggled and it wiggled
There right next to my tongue.

I couldn't bear to pull it.
It sagged. It tipped. It hung.

Then when I ate a carrot,
It popped out into my hand.

I lost a tooth! I lost a tooth!
And I am feeling grand.

Name _____

Story of the Year

The story of the year tells about the four seasons.

In the spring, baby birds and lambs are born.
The days get warmer.
Little plants begin to grow.

Summer brings long days of hot sun.
The garden is full of flowers and bees.
We go to the beach.

In the fall, leaves turn yellow, red, and brown.
They fall from the trees.
We rake them up.

Winter comes and brings the cold.
A bear sleeps.
The lake has a cover of ice.
We have fun in the snow.
We make tracks.

Year after year, the story goes on.
First spring comes, then summer, fall, and winter.

Good Morning!

Wake up! It's morning. What do you see?
　　The sun in the sky
　　And the birds in a tree.

Wake up! It's morning. What do you hear?
　　Someone is singing
　　A song soft and clear.

Wake up! It's morning. What do you hold?
　　The covers around me
　　To keep out the cold.

Wake up! It's morning. What do you smell?
　　Someone is frying
　　An egg, I can tell.

Wake up! It's morning. What do you eat?
　　Warm oats and cold milk,
　　And berries so sweet.

Weather Helps Us

Look outside.
What do you see?
Wind is blowing in the tree.

> Wind helps us.
> It makes sailboats move.
> It makes kites fly high.

Look outside.
What do you see?
Rain is falling on the tree.

> Rain helps us.
> Rain fills lakes and rivers with
> good water.
> Plants need water to live and grow.

Look outside.
What do you see?
The sun is shining on the tree.

> The sun helps us.
> Plants, animals, and people all
> need sunshine.
> The sun helps plants grow.
> People and animals eat plants.

Sing While You Wash

Did you ever sing this song?

"This is the way we wash our hands,
wash our hands, wash our hands.
This is the way we wash our hands,
early in the morning."

Did you know that it's good to sing while you wash?
Here's why! You wash your hands to get rid of germs.
Germs can make you sick. But germs are stubborn! If
you don't wash long enough, the germs will still be
there.

When you wash your hands, scrub them for at least
15 seconds with soap and water. If you sing a song
that you like, you will wash long enough.

Are your hands dirty right now? What song can you
sing while you wash?

Readers' Theater

Page 70 Introduction to Readers' Theater

Page 71 The Colors of Fall*
A script with 9 parts

Page 72 An Insect!
A script with 8 parts

Page 73 Goldilocks and the Three Bears
A script with 8 parts and 4 choruses

Page 79 Jack and the Beanstalk*
A script with 4 parts

* Transparency provided

Readers' Theater

WHAT IS READERS' THEATER?

Readers' Theater is a minimalist way to perform plays. No costumes, props, or scenery are required. Students stand in front of an audience, scripts held in their hands or set on music stands. Very little movement is necessary. Readers' Theater provides the value of performing plays without the logistical considerations.

WHY PERFORM READERS' THEATER?

Readers' Theater yields positive growth in reading skills. Classroom research indicates that students strengthen word recognition, fluency, and comprehension by practicing and performing Readers' Theater selections. In addition, students love to perform, and this enthusiasm carries over to many other aspects of the school day.

HOW DO I START?

Monday

- The teacher introduces or reviews the basics of Readers' Theater.
- Using the transparency copy on the overhead, the teacher reads the play through once, modeling how to read each part.
- The teacher assigns parts, or students volunteer for parts. At first, the teacher should assign parts. As the students gain experience with Readers' Theater procedures and become more fluent readers, they can volunteer or assign parts themselves.

Tuesday through Thursday

- The teacher creates various practice opportunities—individual, group, and home sessions.

Friday

- Select the performance time. Make it a special event, such as a festival on a Friday afternoon.
- Invite an audience. Classmates, another class, parents, or the principal and office staff make good audiences.
- Consider performing for an off-site audience within walking distance.

Name _____

The Colors of Fall

Characters

3 red maple trees

3 orange maple trees

3 yellow maple trees

Red Trees: Fall is as red as a maple leaf.

First Tree: Fall is as red as a chrysanthemum.

Second Tree: Fall is as red as a robin's breast.

Third Tree: Fall is as red as a juicy red apple.

Orange Trees: Fall is as orange as a maple leaf.

Fourth Tree: Fall is as orange as a butterfly weed.

Fifth Tree: Fall is as orange as a monarch butterfly.

Sixth Tree: Fall is as orange as a big orange pumpkin.

Yellow Trees: Fall is as yellow as a maple leaf.

Seventh Tree: Fall is as yellow as goldenrod.

Eighth Tree: Fall is as yellow as a meadowlark.

Ninth Tree: Fall is as yellow as a ripe banana.

Red Trees: Fall is red!

Orange Trees: Fall is orange!

Yellow Trees: Fall is yellow!

All Nine Trees: Fall is FALLING leaves!

Name _____

An Insect!
by Jo Ellen Moore

Characters

Children 1, 2, 3, 4

Grasshopper   **Beetle**

Cricket   **Bumblebee**

Child 1: Eek! An insect!

Grasshopper: Hello! I'm a grasshopper.
I jump high and far on my strong back legs.

Child 2: Eek! An insect!

Beetle: Hello! I'm a beetle.
My wings have a shiny hard cover.

Child 3: Eek! An insect!

Cricket: Hello! I'm a cricket. I rub my wings together.
They make a chirping sound.

Child 4: Eek! An insect!

Bumblebee: Hello! I'm a bumblebee. I fly from flower to flower.
I collect pollen to take back to my hive.

All Children: Wow! There are many kinds of insects!
How are you all alike?

All Insects: We all have 6 legs, antennae, and 3 body parts.
We look different, but we are all still insects.

Building Fluency • EMC 3341 • © Evan-Moor Corp.

Name _____

Goldilocks and the Three Bears
by Leslie Tryon

Characters

Goldilocks	**Baby Bear**	**Goldilocks Chorus**
Mother	**Chair 1**	**Tree Chorus**
Papa Bear	**Chair 2**	**Bee Chorus**
Mama Bear	**Chair 3**	**Flower Chorus**

Goldilocks Chorus: Goldilocks
Wore purple socks
And a big red bow
In her hair.

She knew a dog,
A cat, and a frog;
But had never
Met a bear.

Mother: I'll tie your bow,
Then out you go.
Stay close to the house
And play.

Be a good girl, please.
Don't go near the trees,
Or in your room
You'll stay.

Flower Chorus: Goldilocks is here!
Oh, dear! Oh, dear! Oh, dear!
That bad girl
With the golden hair.

She stomps and skips,
Twirls and trips,
Till our blossoms
And petals are bare.

Tree Chorus: Deep in the trees,
By the pond, where the bees
Hide away
From the bears living there,

In a warm little place
With curtains of lace,
Live Papa, and Mama,
And little Baby Bear.

Mama Bear: The porridge is hot
If it stays in the pot,
So into the bowls
It goes.

It can cool while we talk
And go for a walk.
But right now it's too hot—
Heaven knows.

Goldilocks Chorus: That bad little girl
With the golden curl
Disobeyed her mother;
She did.

She went deep in the trees
To the pond where the bees
Said, "Go back!"
Then quickly they hid.

Building Fluency • EMC 3341 • © Evan-Moor Corp.

Flower Chorus:	She went into the place With the curtains of lace. She didn't even knock Or say please. The table was set With the porridge, and yet There was no one around But those bees.
Bee Chorus:	With no time to waste, She took a quick taste From the big bowl And cried,
Goldilocks:	"It's too hot!"
Bee Chorus:	The next one she tried Made her all cold inside, And she turned up her nose On the spot.
Goldilocks:	My grumbly tummy Wants something real yummy, So I'll try this last bowl And see. I'll just take a bite— Hooray—it's just right! It must have been left Just for me.
Bee Chorus:	Now that her tummy Has had something yummy, She looked for a place To sit down.

A chair with a seat
So high that her feet
Dangle up in the air
Off the ground.

Chair 1: My seat is hard
Like the dirt in the yard,
So I'll thank you to
Sit over there.

Chair 2: My seat is as soft
As the hay in the loft,
It's not right for you
So beware.

Chair 3: Please get off my lap,
And go take your nap
On a bed that you'll find
Over there.

Bee Chorus: The small one was best,
So she took a nice rest.
Before long she lay
Counting sheep.

She heard not a sound
When those bears came around.
She was tucked in the bed
Fast asleep.

Papa Bear: My spoon's in my bowl!
Look out! Heads will roll!
Someone's been eating
My porridge!

Mama Bear: Mine's all wrong, too!
Whatever will I do?
Someone's been eating
My porridge!

Baby Bear: I think that I'll cry
Cause mine's gone bye-bye!
Someone's been here
And they ate all my porridge!

Papa Bear: Hold onto your hat!
If it wasn't the cat,
Then someone's been
Sitting in my chair.

Mama Bear: I just can't believe it!
I may have a snit fit!
Someone's been
Sitting in my chair.

Baby Bear: Well I'm hopping mad!
Someone's really been bad!
They've sat here
And broken my chair.

Tree Chorus: Papa Bear, Mama Bear,
And little Baby Bear,
In a rage to the bedroom
They sped.

Papa Bear cried,
And Mama Bear sighed,
Someone's been sleeping
Right here in my bed.

Baby Bear: Right here in my bed,
Is a big bow of red,
And a girl underneath
With gold hair.

Bee Chorus: Goldilocks' eyes
Opened up with surprise.
She tried, but her legs
Wouldn't go.

Three Bears: Get out of that bed
While you still have a head,
Or we'll eat you—
Right up to your bow!

Tree Chorus: She ran past the bees,
The pond, and the trees,
Past the flowers
As fast as she could.

Her mother was mad
Because she was bad,
But she gave her a hug.
It felt good.

Goldilocks Chorus: Goldilocks
Wore purple socks,
And a big red bow
In her hair.

She knew a dog,
A cat, and a frog,
And now she
Knew three bears.

Building Fluency • EMC 3341 • © Evan-Moor Corp.

Name _____

Jack and the Beanstalk
by Judith Gold and Carrie Mapes
·········· *Characters* ··········

Reader 1	**Reader 2**
Reader 3	**Reader 4**

Reader 1: For Jack and his mother, the times were bad,
So Jack took magic beans for the only cow they had.

Reader 2: Jack's mother was angry and threw with all of her
might. The beans went out the window, and she went
to bed for the night.

Reader 3: Next morning, Jack woke up to find an awesome sight.
A beanstalk had sprouted where the beans lay last
night!

Reader 4: Jack looked up, up, up, as high as eagles fly.
He saw that the beanstalk stretched to the sky.

Reader 1: Jack climbed the beanstalk as quick as a mouse.
There at the top stood a huge stone house!

Reader 2: Inside the castle, Jack crept all around.
He spied a fearsome giant whose voice shook
the ground.

Reader 3: "Fe, fi, fo, fum!" yelled the giant with an angry face. Jack jumped in the oven. What a good hiding place!

Reader 4: From there, Jack saw gold. And since the giant was asleep, Jack ran home fast. The coins were his to keep.

Reader 1: Jack and his mom spent the coins. None remain. So Jack had to climb to the castle again.

Reader 2: Jack crawled through the kitchen, between the table legs. On the table was a hen laying golden eggs.

Reader 3: Jack grabbed the hen and made it home without a hitch. With golden eggs to buy things, now they were rich.

Reader 4: Again Jack climbed the beanstalk, which wasn't too wise. He snatched up a harp as his last golden prize.

Reader 1: As Jack snuck away, the giant woke and said, "I'll catch that little thief! His bones will make my bread!"

Reader 2: The giant gave chase. Down the beanstalk Jack ran fast. He saw his mother and his ax at last.

Reader 3: In the nick of time, Jack made it back. He swung at the beanstalk with a mighty whack.

Reader 4: The giant fell down and Jack laughed with glee. So Jack and his mother lived ever after happily.

Building Fluency • EMC 3341 • © Evan-Moor Corp.